Discover North Calgary's Parks and Green Spaces

David Peyto

Peyto Lake Books

Published by Peyto Lake Books
Calgary, AB
Email info@peytolakebooks.com
Web site www.peytolakebooks.com

Printed and bound in Canada by Blitzprint, Calgary

Copyright 2006 by David Peyto

National Library of Canada Cataloguing in Publication

Peyto, David W.

   Discover North Calgary's parks and green spaces/ David Peyto

ISBN 0-9731066-5-4

Includes bibliographical references

1. Parks--Alberta--Calgary--Guidebooks. 2. Calgary (Alta.)--Guidebooks. I. Title.

FC3697.65.P49 2006   917.123'38   C2006-901993-2

The front cover photos in a clockwise direction from the upper left are of: Bowmont Park, Confederation Park, Hugh Bennett Park and Research Park.
All photos in the book unless otherwise indicated were taken by the author.

Acknowledgements

Thank you to my sisters, Margaret Peyto and Carol Cole, for their support of my self-publishing and for taking the time to edit the books.

Thank you to my brother-in-law Ron Cole and my nephews, Andrew, Ethan and Tim Cole, and my niece, Yolande Cole, for their support.

Thank you to Blitzprint for their assistance with publishing my books.

Thank you to the Glenbow Museum Archives for permission to use the historic photos in this book.

Thank you to Susanah Windrum for her support on the idea for this book.

Thank you to the city parks staff and city archives staff who assisted with my research.

This book is dedicated to Linda. Thank you for your support.

Contents

Introduction

The planning and development of parks and green spaces in Calgary began just ten years after the North West Mounted Police arrived in 1875 and constructed a fort at the confluence of the Bow and Elbow Rivers.

In 1885 the Dominion Lands Board established a Calgary office. William Pearce, a member of this board, played a part in the decision to reserve areas of land for park purposes for the people of Calgary as a gift from the Canadian Government. The first area of land set aside that same year was located at 12th Avenue and 4th Street SW. Over the next few years this land was developed and given the name Central Park. Today the park is known as Central Memorial Park.

A second area of land to the west of the town and adjacent to the Bow River was also reserved for park use. This area on 9th Avenue west of 11th Street SW was to become known as Mewata Park. Today that park has undergone major changes from its early years and is now best known to Calgarians as Shaw Millennium Park.

The year 1890 saw the first formal park being established in Calgary when the Canadian Pacific Railway created a public park adjacent to the railway station.

Today Calgary has grown from that small town of a few hundred people to a large city of approximately one million people. As the population of Calgary has grown the number of city parks and green spaces has greatly increased.

The parks department of the city has done a tremendous job of developing these parks and green spaces over the years. The creation of some parks was made possible through donations of land by generous Calgarians. Other parks have developed as a result of the foresight and hard work of citizens. In some parts of the city developers have set aside land which has been converted to parks and green space.

Using this book

This book is a guide for the reader to discover many of the parks and green spaces in northwest and northeast Calgary. In the book the parks and green spaces in North Calgary have been grouped into five areas using some of the major roads as boundaries for the areas.

The locations described in the book include the major multi-use parks and the larger athletic parks. The book also includes ravines, escarpments, wetland ponds and green spaces adjacent to the Bow River. Some of the older community parks and playgrounds are also mentioned. The reader is given information on the facilities and activities available in each park and green space. Some of the locations in this book have been called green spaces as they don't appear to have an official park name.

A brief history of some of the older parks and any historic buildings adjacent to these parks is also included. The University of Calgary and SAIT are included because of the park-like setting of both campuses. Directions are given for visiting the parks and green spaces when using your own vehicle or when using public transit.

This book is the first in a three volume series on Calgary's Parks and Green Spaces. The other two books to be published are *Discover Southeast Calgary's Parks and Green Spaces* and *Discover Southwest Calgary's Parks and Green Spaces*. These two books should be published by late 2007.

You are invited to discover the parks and green spaces of North Calgary. Enjoy yourself. As you explore North Calgary you might even discover some little park or green space not included in this book.

Area One

Area one is on the west and south sides of Crowchild Trail from the Bow River to the city's western boundary. The area's communities are Bowness, Montgomery, Parkdale, St. Andrews Heights, Scenic Acres, Silver Springs, Tuscany, University Heights, University of Calgary, Valley Ridge, Varsity Acres and Varsity Estates.

"This park is becoming more popular each year as a picnic resort, some thousands of people having visited it during the season. People go there with the idea of getting into the country ... it seems to me it is not a park to be developed into intensive recreational use, but should be so maintained as to give all the sense of freedom that the unspoiled country gives."
- William Reader, Calgary Parks Superintendent, 1913 - referring to Bowness Park.

Bowness Park Lagoon

9

Area One Map

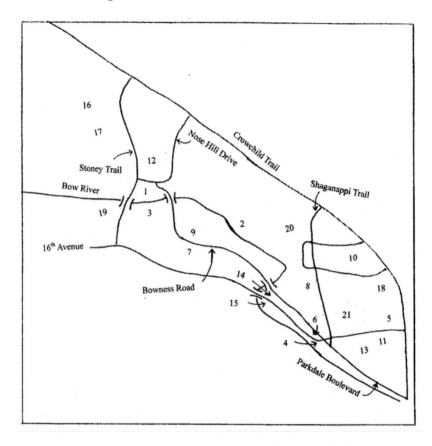

1. Baker Park
2. Bowmont Park
3. Bowness Park
4. Bow River Pathway - Home Road to Crowchild
5. Foothills Athletic Park
6. George R. Gell Park
7. MacIntosh Park
8. Montalban Avenue Green Space
9. Queen Elizabeth Park
10. Research Park
11. St Andrews Park
12. Scenic Acres Pathway
13. Shagnessey Heights Park
14. Shouldice Park
15. Shouldice Athletic Park
16. Tuscany Green Space
17. Twelve Mile Coulee
18. University of Calgary
19. Valley Ridge Escarpment
20. Varsity Ravine Pathway
21. West Campus Pond Park

Baker Park

Scenic Bow Road NW
Bus: 40
Cycling, In-Line Skating, Picnic Tables, Walking, Washrooms (Seasonal)

Description:
The site of this park was the former location of the Baker Memorial Sanatorium buildings. Today Baker Park stretches along the north side of the Bow River just west of the 85th Street Bridge. To date only a portion of the park area has been formally developed.

Wildflower Mount in Baker Park

Several maps in the park show the rather formal layout of the site. Names such as: The Commons, Wildflower Mount, The Sunbowl and Scenic Bow Arbour have been given to locations within the park. Wildflower Mount adjacent to the main parking lot has a set of steps leading up to a gazebo-like structure. The Sunbowl is a sunken semi-circular area adjacent to the river. There are paths around the edge of and cutting across The Sunbowl. A prominent feature in this area is the large blocks of sandstone on which park visitors can sit and relax while watching bird activity on the river.

Visitors can take a walk along the paved Bow River Pathway which passes through the entire length of the park. Cyclists riding along the pathway and looking for a pleasant rest area may want to stop at The Sunbowl.

On a hot weekend afternoon when Bowness Park across the river is overflowing with picnickers, this park might be considered as an alternate location for a visit.

Central Alberta Sanatorium, Keith district, Calgary, Alberta, 1926. (Glenbow Archives NA-2910-13)

History:
The Baker Memorial Sanatorium, formerly located on this site, served as a treatment centre for tuberculosis patients from 1920 to the 1970s. The centre's namesake, Dr. A.H. Baker, was the sanatorium's director from 1920 to 1950. The facility was later used as a treatment centre for mentally handicapped children and adults. The buildings were demolished in the 1980s.

Nearby Parks and Green Spaces:

Bowness Park is directly across the river from Baker Park and can be reached by going west along the paved path and crossing the pedestrian bridge under Stoney Trail or by heading east on the path to the 85th Street Bridge. Valley Ridge Escarpment is at the west end of Bowness Park near the Stoney Trail Bridge. Bowmont Park is east of the 85th Street Bridge on the same side of the river as Baker Park.

The Sunbowl area of Baker Park

Bowmont Park

Middle area of the park: Silver Springs Boulevard and 54th Avenue NW
Bus: 37/137, 43/143
West end of the park: 85th Street Bridge
Bus: 40
East end of the park: 40th Avenue and 53rd Street NW or 52nd Street west of Home Road NW
Bus: 37/137, 43/143, 22/122, 9, 408
Bird Watching, Cycling, Natural Area, Views, Walking

Description:

This large natural environment park is on the north side of the Bow River adjacent to the southern edge of the districts of Silver Springs and Varsity Estates. The park area includes escarpment slopes, three ravines, the flat areas along the top of the escarpments and some flat areas at the base of the slopes beside the Bow River. There are houses facing the roads that are along the top of the escarpments. The Bow River Pathway runs the entire length of the park, a distance of about 6 km. A trip along the path from one end of the park to the other end can be challenging with several ascents and descents of the escarpments.

Description of the middle area of the park:

Park users starting a visit to the park at 54th Avenue and Silver Springs Boulevard have several route options. One choice is to head south from the parking area and follow the trail along the top of the escarpment beside Silverview Drive. Along this road there are several trails leading down the escarpment.

Near the north end of Silverview Drive there is a path junction that offers more route options. The left branch of the path at the junction can be followed on a long descent of the escarpment down towards the river. At the bottom of the escarpment the paved path can be followed to the east end of the park. There are also trails along the base of the escarpment and trails leading to the river bank.

The right branch of the path at this junction descends down into the park's middle ravine which is known locally as *Waterfall Valley*. In the ravine a dirt trail leads down the ravine towards the river from the paved path. At the end of this trail there is a small waterfall and a viewing platform overlooking the river.

You can also climb up the paved path on the west side of the ravine and walk along the top of the escarpment beside Silver Crest Drive. The main path then veers to the left away from the road and begins a steep descent down the escarpment into the west ravine (described in the west end of the park). From the top of the escarpment slopes there are good views. Look for the large Bow River island that is part of the park. This is a great location for birds as there is no bridge to the island.

At the Waterfall Valley viewpoint in the middle ravine

Description of the west end of the park:

At the west end of the park there are three parking areas just east of 85th Street. One of the parking areas is on the north side of 85th Street bridge just south of the railway tracks. On the north side of the railway tracks there are two parking areas along a gravel road. The west end of the park is very popular with dog walkers.

From the parking lot south of the tracks the paved path can be followed west to the 85th Street bridge or east towards the CPR bridge. Just before reaching the train bridge a path leads to the right across a small bridge onto an island and then across the Bowmont Pedestrian Bridge into the district of Bowness. On the east side of the train bridge the path crosses the gravel road leading to one of the other parking lots. After crossing the road the path leads to the bottom end of the west ravine. From here there are stairs leading up the escarpment on the west side of the ravine and a steep path leading up the escarpment on the east side of the ravine, (This path leads to the middle area of the park). A path also leads up the ravine to Silver Springs Road.

Pathway in the west ravine of Bowmont Park

Description of the east end of the park:

At the east end of the park there is parking along the

16

south side of 40th Avenue just west of 53rd Street. Also at the east end of the park there is a parking lot on 52nd Street just west of Home Road. At the east end of the park there is a privately owned gravel pit operation within the boundaries of the park.

Park visitors at the east end of the park alongside 40th Avenue can follow trails west along the top of the escarpment overlooking the gravel pit. At the west end of 40th Avenue, several trails lead down into the east ravine of the park. From there trails lead up the escarpment on the west side of the ravine. Another trail heads west along the base of the escarpment and joins the Bow River Pathway. There are also trails leading south towards the river pathway. The river pathway can be followed to the left between the gravel pit fence and the river to reach the parking lot beside 52nd Street. From here trails lead to the top of the escarpment beside the intersection of 32nd Avenue and Home Road. From there walk along the top of the escarpment back to 40th Avenue.

History:

The site of Bowmont Park was once part of the Cochrane Ranche property. The Cochrane Ranche Company was the first of many large ranches in Western Canada. The company leased over one hundred thousand acres. In 1881 the first cattle were purchased by the company. Senator Matthew H. Cochrane of Quebec was the president of the company.

An early resident living in the area north of the park called it Silver Springs, after a location in Florida. John Black farmed in this area until 1946. He called the area "Glen Carse" after a locality in his native Scotland.

Nearby Parks and Green Spaces:

At the west end of the park the paved Bow River Pathway goes under the 85th Street Bridge and continues west to Baker Park. Another option is to cross the 85th Street Bridge to reach Bowness Park. From the parking lot on 52nd Street, Shouldice Park is at the bottom of the hill on the far side of Bowness Road.

Bowness Park

48th Avenue and 88th Street NW
Bus: 1, 40
Amusement Rides, Barbeque Stands, Bird Watching, Canoeing, Concession, Fire Pits, Miniature Train, Mini-Golf, Paddleboats, Picnic Tables, Picnic Shelters, Playgrounds, Skating, Wading Pool, Walking, Washrooms.

Lagoon and fountain at Bowness Park

Description:
Are you planning a large family or group picnic? Bowness Park might be the ideal location. For many years Bowness Park has been one of Calgary's most popular family parks. In the warmer weather hundreds of people congregate here beside the Bow River for picnics. There are several picnic shelters which can be reserved for groups. Numerous barbeque stands and fire pits are scattered throughout the park for visitors bringing food to

cook at their picnic.

Park users in the summer can choose from a wide variety of activities. Little children will enjoy riding around the east end of the park on the miniature train or spending some time on the amusement rides. Older park users can try a round of mini-golf or rent one of the canoes or paddleboats and explore the lagoon or canal. A spray pool area is also very popular on hot summer days. There are also open grass areas for impromptu ball games or a game of croquet or bocce.

In the winter Bowness still attracts large numbers of visitors. Skaters head to the park for an enjoyable afternoon of gliding around the lagoon and then huddling around one of the fire pits to warm up.

Civic Picnic, Bowness Park, Calgary, ca. 1910s
(Glenbow Archives NA-2399-10)

The park road which circles through the park makes it easier for anyone with restricted mobility to access the picnic areas which are located close to the road.

There are several route options for walking in the park. One choice is to follow the trail beside the river to the west end of the park below the Stoney Trail Bridge and then return along the trail beside the canal back to your starting point. From below the bridge there is access to a short trail on the south side of the canal in an area known as the Wood's Douglas Fir Tree Sanctuary. This area was designated as a provincial historic resource in 1990. Some of the trees in this area are over 400 years old. The location is one of only three Douglas Fir stands within Calgary.

Another route choice is to follow the paved trail beside the lagoon. The waterfowl in the lagoon are often very bold as they approach visitors looking for a handout. Please refrain from feeding the waterfowl as it is a detrimental activity. Fed waterfowl can become too dependent on humans for supplying their food.

If you are looking for a quieter place to walk head to the east end of the park towards the 85th Street bridge. From here a dirt trail leads under the bridge and into an undeveloped area of the park with trails amongst the trees.

History:

In 1911 the city of Calgary accepted Bowness resident John Hextall's offer to acquire the area that is now Bowness Park. In exchange the city extended the street railway line from Calgary to the park. The street railway took over the operation of the park in 1917.

Canoeing in the park started in 1918. In the 1920s numerous facilities were added to the park. These included a picnic pavilion, a swimming pool, a merry-go-round (this is now in Heritage Park), summer cottages which park visitors could rent, a dance hall and a concession. Later additions to the park were a shooting gallery, the miniature railway, pony rides and some amusement rides. The first fountain in the lagoon operated from 1927 until the late 1960s. The Parks

Foundation installed the present fountain in 1988.

By the late 1940s the cottages were demolished. The pool closed in 1959 and this was followed by the closure of the dance hall the following year. When Bowness was annexed by Calgary in the early 1960s the city took over the operation of the park.

Nearby Parks and Green Spaces:

The Valley Ridge Escarpment is adjacent to the west end of the park beside the Stoney Trail Bridge. Baker Park is directly across the river from Bowness Park and can be reached by either crossing the Stoney Trail Pedestrian Bridge or the 85th Street Bridge. Bowmont Park can be reached by heading east on the north side of the 85th Street Bridge.

Swimming at Bowness Park, Calgary, August 1930
(Glenbow Archives ND-8-338)

21

Bow River Pathway - Home Road to Crowchild Trail

Shaganappi Trail & Bowness Road NW
Bus: 1, 40
Cycling, In-line Skating, Walking

Description:
This section of the Bow River Pathway from Home Road to Crowchild Trail is flat. Most of this section of pathway is twinned with runners and walkers using the path closer to the river. In the winter only the path used by cyclists and in-line skaters is usually cleared of snow. There is a large parking lot which can be accessed from the intersection of Shaganappi Trail and Bowness Road. This parking lot is a very popular location for people to leave their vehicles and commute to work downtown by bike or in-line skates. This green space is also very popular with dog walkers.

The Bow River near the south end of Home Road

The Point McKay washroom building is beside this parking lot. In the warmer weather the concession beside the parking lot is open for anyone looking for a coffee or snack while using the pathway. From this parking lot you can also cross the Harry Boothman pedestrian bridge to Edworthy Park. Mr. Boothman was the superintendent and director of Calgary Parks and Recreation from 1961 to 1976. He was a huge advocate for the development of the pathway system throughout the city.

Heading west on the path from the parking lot, you can follow the green space beside the river as far as Home Road at the southeast corner of Shouldice Athletic Park. The Bow River Pathway continues west along the south side of the athletic park. There are two parking lots on Home Road.

Looking towards downtown Calgary from 37th Street and Parkdale Boulevard

Heading east on the pathway from the main parking

lot you pass a small parking lot at 37th Street and Parkdale Boulevard. As you approach Crowchild Trail the two paths join and you enter a very narrow section where the traffic of Parkdale Boulevard is right beside the path.

There are numerous benches beside the river to sit and relax on while watching the activity around you, whether it be the waterfowl and birds along the river, pathway users, people floating down the river or trains on the other side of the river.

Nearby Parks and Green Spaces:
Shouldice Athletic Park and the Bow River Pathway from Crowchild Trail to Centre Street are connected to this section of pathway. The Douglas Fir Trail, Lawrey Gardens and Edworthy Park are across the river from this section of pathway. These parks will be included in the Southwest parks and green spaces book.

Foothills Athletic Park
2431 Crowchild Trail NW
Bus 9, 20, 72/73
Arenas, Athletics Track, Ball Diamond, Baseball Stadium, Football Stadium, Indoor Pool, Soccer Fields, Tennis Courts, Volleyball

Description:
The most prominent facility in this park is McMahon Stadium whose principal tenant is the Calgary Stampeders Football Club. The stadium was the venue for the Opening and Closing Ceremonies of the 1988 Winter Olympics. It was named for brothers Frank and George McMahon who made a donation in 1960 to begin the construction of the stadium. The Red and White Club, a multi-purpose facility, is adjacent to the north end of the stadium.

Burns Stadium, Calgary's premier baseball stadium, is situated at the northeast corner of the park beside 24th Avenue and Crowchild Trail. On the 24th Avenue side of the park is a covered volleyball facility, tennis courts and Foothills swimming pool. There are two ice arenas in the northwest corner of the park adjacent to University Drive. The Father David Bauer Arena is named for the Roman Catholic priest who played a key role in the formation of a Canadian national hockey team in 1962. The second arena is named for Norma Bush. She was a Calgary nurse who was very active in sports and community activities. Norma's interests included the Calalta Figure Skating Club, fastball, basketball and hockey. The other facilities in the park include an athletic track, ball diamonds, and soccer fields.

Nearby Parks and Green Spaces:
The University of Calgary is located directly north of Foothills Athletic Park.

George R. Gell Park
16th Avenue and 43rd Street NW
Bus: 1, 40
Playground

Description:
A visit to this small neighbourhood park can be disturbed by the noise of traffic on the very busy 16th Avenue NW (Trans Canada Highway) which runs along the south side of the park. A playground is located in the park. This park seems to have very few visitors, possibly because of its location.

History:
The park is located on the former site of the Gell family home. George Gell arrived in Calgary in 1910 from England. He first worked in real estate before seeking employment with the Calgary Board of Education. He began work in the stores area for the Board and by 1941 had become secretary-treasurer of the Board. The park was named for Mr. Gell in 1982.

Nearby Parks and Green Spaces:

At the southwest corner of the park a flashing pedestrian light can be used to cross 16th Avenue. The Bow River Pathway from Home Road to Crowchild Trail is just a short walk from the pedestrian crossing.

Looking south across 16th Avenue towards Edworthy Park from George R. Gell Park

MacIntosh Park

37th Avenue NW between 74th and 76th Streets
Bus: 1, 40
Commemorative Plaque, Playground

Description:

Most visitors to this park are probably neighbourhood children. This small community park is between houses on 37th Avenue. Visitors to the park may want to pause and reflect for a few moments in front of the large stone memorial located in the southwest corner of this small neighbourhood park. The stone is inscribed as the

Bowness Children's Memorial. It is dedicated to the memory of nine children who used to play in this park. There are no dates or other information on the memorial. Across the other side of the park from the stone memorial is a playground.

Bowness Children's Memorial

Montalban Avenue Green Space

Montalban Avenue and 48th Street NW
Bus: 10
Views, Walking

Description:
This large open community green space extends along an escarpment from 48th Street to Mackay Road. From the top edge of the escarpment there is a great view towards Edworthy Park, Canada Olympic Park and the mountains. The south or lower end of the escarpment is adjacent to 23rd Avenue. From here the grass slope rises steeply to the top end of the green space beside

Montalban Avenue, Montalban Drive and Montalban Crescent. There are benches along the top edge of the escarpment for those wanting to just sit and enjoy the view.

Looking west in Montalban Park

Queen Elizabeth Park

77th Street and 41st Avenue NW
Bus: 1
Commemorative Area, Playground

Description:
A sign indicates that this small triangular-shaped neighbourhood park is maintained jointly by the Royal Canadian Legion Branch 268 and City Parks/Recreation Department. A memorial stone surrounded by a chain fence is dedicated to the memory of those who gave their lives in military service.

In the northwest corner of the park there is a second stone with a plaque to commemorate the coronation of

Queen Elizabeth in 1953. The only other facility in the park is a playground.

Memorial Cairn in Queen Elizabeth Park

Research Park
40th Avenue and 37th Street NW
Bus: 9
Bird Watching, Fitness Circuit, Playground, Rest Area

Description:
Hidden away in the northwest corner of University Research Park is this impressive little park. The main feature of the park is a small pond that often attracts waterfowl. The water is drained from the pond in the winter. There are benches and a gazebo near the water. Water for the pond comes out of several pipes on the north side of the park.

The stations of a fitness circuit are located around the perimeter of the park. There is also a small playground. The park is a great location to relax and watch the waterfowl.

Research Park

St. Andrews Park

University Drive and 13th Avenue NW
Bus: 9, 72/73
Ball Diamonds, Community Hall, Playground, Soccer Fields, Tennis Courts, Tobogganing

Description:
If anyone is looking for a new toboggan hill this may be the location to visit. The wide and reasonably steep hill at the north end of the park has long been a favourite spot for Calgary's toboggan enthusiasts.

Please note that there is very limited parking at the top of the hill so it is suggested that you use the main parking lot on 13th Avenue and then walk across the playing fields to the hill.

In summer the hill is deserted as park visitors make use of the other facilities in the park.

Toboggan hill in St. Andrews Community Park

Scenic Acres Pathway

Scenic Acres Drive just west of Scimitar Point NW
Bus: 37/137, 43/143
Ball Diamond, Natural Area, Playground, Soccer Fields,
Tennis Courts, Walking

Description:
This pathway is in a great location as it wanders through a narrow strip of green space beside a small creek. The suggested location to park is on Scenic Acres Drive near the tennis courts. From here walkers can head south or north on the paved path.

The south path leads into a very shallow ravine that is partially treed. The sound of running water can soon be heard as the water flows out of a pipe and wends its way down through the ravine. The water was still running

31

with very little ice buildup during the mild weather in January 2006. Several paths join the main path. The path can be followed as far as a tunnel leading under Stoney Trail. The paved path ends at the Scenic Acres side of the tunnel.

Small creek along the south end of the path

The north path leads gradually uphill across an open area past tennis courts, playing fields and a playground before entering a partially treed shallow ravine. This area also has a creek which starts near the north end of the ravine and ends up flowing underground just north of Scenic Acres Drive. On a walk through this area in January 2006, there was a great deal more ice here than in the south section of the walk. At Scenic Park Gate the path leaves the ravine area.

Nearby:
Twelve Mile Coulee can be reached by going to the end of the south path and traveling through the tunnel under Stoney Trail.

The north section of the path

Shagnessey Heights Park
8th Avenue and 29th Street NW
Bus: 20, 40
Views, Walking

Description:
This escarpment area is located on the south side of St Andrews Heights between 29th Street and Crowchild Trail. Numerous trails can be followed across the escarpment slope.

Parking may be a problem as the overflow of vehicles from the Foothills Medical Centre often occupies 8th Avenue along the bottom edge of the park or Toronto Crescent along the top of the escarpment. There are also parking restrictions at the west end of Toronto Crescent. A walk along the top of the escarpment beside Toronto Crescent offers a great panoramic view. There are benches beside Toronto Crescent for those wanting to sit and enjoy the view.

Looking west from the top of the escarpment

Shouldice Park

Bowness Road and 52nd Street NW
Bus: 1, 40
Ball Diamond, Barbeque Stands, Cycling, Indoor Pool,
Picnic , Playground, Soccer Field, Tennis Courts,
Walking, Washrooms

Description:
    This park beside the Bow River is an excellent location
for a picnic. Although the park is sandwiched between
two busy roads, 16th Avenue (Trans Canada Highway) and
Bowness Road, it is still worth the visit. The picnic tables
are located close to the Bow River beside the path.
    The park facilities include the Shouldice Indoor Pool
and some tennis courts. On the east side of the park
there is a soccer field and a ball diamond. The Bow River
Pathway runs along the west side of the park beside the

river.

Shouldice Park picnic area

History:

The family of James and Mary Shouldice settled in Calgary in 1901. About 10 years later, James and his neighbour Alfred S. MacKay donated 100 acres to the city of Calgary for use as a park. This donation was under the condition that the city extend the street railway as far as the bridge over the river. If you walk to the Bowness Road side of the park there are several historic plaques which have been placed on the former traffic bridge that has now been converted for pedestrian and cycle use only.

This bridge was constructed in 1910/11. It was first used by pedestrians, horses and carts. The Municipal Railway line started using the bridge in 1912 to cross the river on the way to Bowness Park. The adjacent traffic bridge was constructed in the 1980s.

Nearby Parks and Green Spaces:

Shouldice Athletic Park is located on the south side of

the Trans Canada Highway. The east end of Bowmont Park is a short distance up 52nd Street from Bowness Road.

John Hextall Bridge

Shouldice Athletic Park

1515 Home Road NW
Bus: 1, 40
Arena, Ball Diamonds, Community Hall, Cycling, Football Fields, Soccer Fields, Walking

Description:
This large athletic park is located adjacent to the Bow River. The park has numerous ball diamonds, soccer and football fields. Football enthusiasts might want to consider a visit here in the fall to watch Calgary's high school players in action.

In the northeast corner of the park there is a community hall and an arena. The paved Bow River Pathway runs along the south side of the park.

Nearby Parks and Green Spaces:
Shouldice Park is located on the other side of 16th Avenue if park users are looking for a picnic spot after a game in the park. The Bow River Pathway from Home Road to Crowchild Trail extends east from the southeast corner of the park.

Shouldice Athletic Park playing fields

Tuscany Green Space
Tuscany Valley View and Tuscany Drive NW
Bus: 421
Cycling, Natural Area, Walking

Description:
The suggested parking spot for exploring the green space in Tuscany is on the east side of Tuscany Valley View near where it meets Tuscany Drive. This green space has been divided into three areas to explore. From the starting point one path leads north and climbs a slope on the east side of Tuscany Valley View. This path

ends at some playing fields. There is a good view from the top of the slope.

Creek crossing area in the ravine

Another route is to head west from Tuscany Valley View following a path that skirts a dry pond. A small creek flows beside this path. In the winter there is a huge build up of ice beside this path. The path then starts to head in a northwestly direction, passing a small wetlands. After crossing Tusslewood Drive the path wanders past two small ponds and then heads along one side of a heavily treed area located between houses. At the time of writing the path just ends but may be extended as the northwest corner of the community is developed.

The third route to follow from the starting point is much more of an adventure. On the east side of Tuscany Valley View look for a dirt trail that can be followed south through a treed ravine. Be forewarned that as you follow this trail you may get your shoes wet. The trail crosses the small creek without the use of a bridge. After crossing the creek the trail climbs up out of the ravine and ends at the west side of a dry pond, on the north side of Tuscany Boulevard.

Nearby Parks and Green Spaces:
Twelve Mile Coulee is on the south side of Tuscany Boulevard at Tuscany Hills Road.

Twelve Mile Coulee
Tuscany Boulevard & Tuscany Hills Road
Bus: 421
Bird Watching, Cycling, Natural Area, Sculpture, Walking

Twelve Mile Coulee looking north

Description:
This natural area is a great place to explore. Children

should enjoy a walk through the coulee. Stoney Trail is on the east side. The houses on the eastern edge of Tuscany south of Tuscany Drive back onto the coulee. A paved path behind these houses follows the top edge of the escarpment. Along this path is a sculpture entitled *Sunning Buffalo* by artist Eric Peterson. From the location of the sculpture there are stairs leading down the escarpment.

Twelve Mile Coulee looking south

The coulee trail crosses over the small creek several times so it may be difficult to keep footwear dry and clean. In the winter there may be a build up of ice in the bottom of the coulee. As houses are built at the south end of the district, it seems likely that the paved path will probably be extended further south along the top of the escarpment.

There are several trails where walkers can climb up or down the escarpment between the paved path and the bottom of the coulee. There are also trails that climb up the escarpment on the east side of the coulee. Trails can be followed along the top of the east side escarpment next to Stoney Trail.

Nearby:
At the south end of the coulee a dirt trail can be followed towards Stoney Trail. The trail goes through a tunnel under the road and connects with the Scenic Acres Pathway. The Tuscany Green Space is located on Tuscany Valley View just north of the suggested starting location for Twelve Mile Coulee.

University of Calgary
University Way NW
Bus: 9, 19, 20, 72/73
Playing Fields, Rest Area, Sculptures

Swann Mall

Description:
The University of Calgary is not a city park, but it does have several green spaces scattered throughout the

campus. Visitors to the campus will need to pay for parking.

One area to visit is Swann Mall, a green area between the MacKimmie Library Tower and the University Administration Building. There is a small pond and several sculptures to be found in this area. *Untitled Steel Sculpture* by George Norris is at the top of a small rise. There is also a steel sculpture entitled *Garden of Learning* by Katie Ohe in this area.

Another pleasant green space is in front of the MacEwan Student Centre. In this area there is a sculpture entitled *Olympic Arch* by Colette Whitten and Paul Kipps. It features eight life-size bronze figures supporting an arch.

Olympic Arch

Other sculptures can be found in front of the Engineering building and around the edges of Craigie Hall. On the east side of the campus near the path leading to the C-Train Station is *Magyar Centennial Gateway*, dedicated to the Hungarian immigrants who have made Canada their home. *Spire* by Bob Boyce is a large sculpture near the north entrance to the Olympic Oval. Near this sculpture is one of the Olympic cauldrons.

There are several playing fields located on the west side of the campus.

Nearby Parks and Green Spaces:
Foothills Athletic Park is located south of 24th Avenue, adjacent to the south side of the campus. At the southwest corner of the campus on 24th Avenue, a paved path leads south from near the physical plant building into West Campus Pond Park.

Valley Ridge Escarpment
West end of Bowness Park
Bus: 1
Natural area, Views, Walking

Description:
This natural area is a heavily treed north-facing escarpment located adjacent to the west end of Bowness Park. A paved path and a dirt trail both start at the bottom of the escarpment, underneath the massive structure of the Stoney Trail Bridge. At the top of the escarpment the paved path can be followed behind the houses along the north side of the Valley Ridge district. There are several paths leading into the district. There are excellent views to the north along this path. Please note that the escarpment can be very icy during the winter months.

Nearby Parks and Green Spaces:
Bowness Park is adjacent to the east end of the escarpment. Baker Park can be reached by going across the Stoney Trail pedestrian bridge and heading east a

short distance.

Trail leading down Valley Ridge Escarpment

Varsity Ravine Pathway

Varsity Estates Drive & 53rd Street NW
Bus: 10, 22/122, 37/137, 43/143
Cycling, Playground, Tobogganing, Walking

Description:
On 53rd Street just south of Varsity Estates Drive, a paved path leads east and then north through a shallow ravine. The path then follows an overpass to cross Crowchild Trail. This path can be followed north through Dalhousie and across John Laurie Boulevard into Edgemont.

At the south end of the ravine there is a good toboggan hill. On the east side of the ravine there is a small playground near the south end of Viceroy Drive.

Varsity Ravine Pathway

West Campus Pond Park

24th Avenue & West Campus Drive NW
Bus: 9
Bird Watching, Views, Rest Area, Walking

Description:
Parking is very restricted at the north end of this park near 24th Avenue. The best option is to park along the edge of an ornamental park on Ungava Road and then walk over to Utah Drive. A paved path leads from this road, between houses and then across an alley to a gateway on the east side of the park. A paved path leads north through the park to connect with university paths at 24th Avenue.

There is an excellent view to the west from this park.

There are benches close to the edge of the pond and usually some waterfowl to watch.

Nearby Parks and Green Spaces:
This park is located adjacent to the southwest corner of the University of Calgary campus.

West Campus Pond looking northwest towards the Children's Hospital

Area Two

The boundaries of this area are north of Crowchild Trail and west of Shaganappi Trail, extending as far as the city limits. The districts in area two are Arbour Lake, Citadel, Dalhousie, Edgemont, Hamptons, Hawkwood, Ranchlands, Rocky Ridge, Royal Oak and Sherwood.

"Parks are the breathing lungs and beating hearts of great cities ... and in them are whispers of peace and joy."
- J.T. Ronald, Mayor of Seattle, 1892-93

Edgemont Path east of Edgemont Ravine

Area Two Map

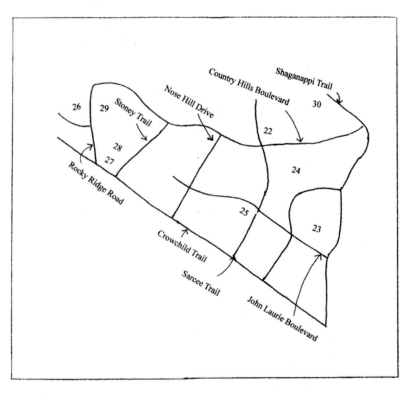

22. Citadel and Hamptons Pathway
23. Edgemont Escarpment
24. Edgemont Ravines
25. Ranch Estates Drive Green Space
26. Rocky Ridge Ranch Wetlands
27. Royal Oak Drive Wetlands
28. Royal Oak Ravine
29. Royal Oak Way Wetland
30. Sherwood Pathway

Citadel and Hamptons Pathway

Hamptons Boulevard and Hampshire Gate
Bus: 54/154
Playground, Tennis Courts, Walking

Description:

A paved path leads through the west side of Hamptons to a small ravine located between Hamptons and Citadel. A walk along this path begins at the ornamental gateway on Hamptons Boulevard. The path leads north and then crosses Hamptons Boulevard and follows a green space between houses to a fence for the Country Club of the Hamptons. The path leads down into the shallow ravine and soon ends at the houses in Citadel on the west side of the ravine.

Pathway in the ravine between Citadel and Hamptons

Edgemont Escarpment

Edenwold Road and Edenstone Road NW
Bus: 77
Views, Walking

Description:

This is a green space with terrific views. From the starting location there are two walking route options. The west loop heads in a southwesterly direction along one of the many trails on the escarpment. The route goes around behind the houses on Edenstone View and then heads north as far as Edgemont Boulevard. From here turn right and then make another right turn onto Edenwold Drive and follow it back to the starting point. As the route heads north there is a great view west towards the mountains.

View from Edgemont Escarpment

The east loop heads in a southeasterly direction across the escarpment passing behind the houses at the south end of Edelweiss Point. The route then heads

50

north. There is a view to the east of Nose Hill Park on the far side of Shaganappi Trail. Just north of Edelweiss Crescent turn left onto Edenwold Drive and follow the road back to the starting point.

Nearby Parks and Green Spaces:
On the west loop along the escarpment the Edgemont Ravines path begins just west of Edgemont Boulevard on Edgepark Boulevard.

Edgemont Ravines
Edgepark Boulevard and Edgebyne Crescent NW
Bus: 54/154, 77
Bird Watching, Cycling, Natural Area, Playground, Sculpture, Tennis , Walking

The first ravine near the jackrabbit sculptures

Description:
A summer visit to the wetlands area at dusk gives the visitor the experience of hearing the sound of the various

birds falling silent as darkness settles across the park.

The paved path leads through a natural area featuring two adjoining ravines. In the first ravine the route starts near some tennis courts and heads in a roughly northerly direction. Look for the sculpture of three jackrabbits near the playground. Near the high point of the path there is a gazebo, a small pond and an ornamental waterfall flowing into the pond. From here the path continues north to a major pathway junction just south of Country Hills Boulevard.

Take the right branch as it leads down into a wider and deeper ravine than the first ravine. Near the bottom of the ravine the path goes by an excellent wetlands area. Several different birds and waterfowl can usually be seen in this area.

Wetlands in the second ravine

Nearby Parks and Green Spaces:

From the starting point on Edgebyne Crescent the Edgemont Escarpment can be seen just to the east across Shaganappi Trail. From the bottom of the ravine by the wetlands there is a path that continues on the east side of Edgebrook Boulevard past some ball diamonds and through a tunnel under Shaganappi Trail and into the northwest corner of MacEwan. This path can then be followed through a second tunnel under Country Hills Boulevard to connect with the Hidden Valley Pathway.

Ranch Estates Drive Green Space
Ranch Estates Drive and Ranch Estates Road NW
Bus: 37/137, 76
Views, Walking

View looking towards the southeast

Description:
This hilly green space with a mix of open spaces and trees in the northeast corner of Ranchlands is very popular with dog walkers. There are several gravel trails through the area. From the high points of the area there are excellent views.

Rocky Ridge Ranch Wetlands

Rocky Ridge Landing NW
Bus: 426
Bird Watching, Playground, Walking

Description:
This park features a short walking route of a few hundred metres around the edge of a small wetlands. There are paved and gravel sections along the path. Rocky Ridge Road is along the east side of the wetlands. There are trees and houses along the walking route on the other three sides. On several visits here waterfowl were observed in the water. There is a playground on the south side of the wetlands.

Rocky Ridge Ranch Wetlands

Royal Oak Drive Wetlands

Royal Oak Drive just west of 100 Royal Crest Bay
Bus: 426
Bird Watching, Walking

Description:
A walking route of about 1 kilometre around this wetlands changes from a paved path to a dirt trail. The wetlands has one large pond and several smaller ponds. A gazebo-like structure with benches allows visitors to sit and watch the waterfowl.

Royal Oak Drive Wetlands

Those making a complete circuit of the wetlands should use caution on the dirt trails as the surface is uneven and in some places it is necessary to step on large rocks. This area is an excellent location for observing birds.

Nearby Parks and Green Spaces:
From the starting point you can cross Royal Oak Drive and follow the paved path leading past a playground and into Royal Oak Ravine.

Royal Oak Ravine

Royal Oak Drive just west of 100 Royal Crest Bay
Bus: 426
Playground, Walking

Description:
The route through this ravine goes in a northwesterly direction and ends near Royal Abbey Rise. The paved path starts near a playground and soon splits. The right branch continues along the top of the slope on the east side of the ravine. The left branch soon turns into a dirt trail. On the left branch a small pond is soon passed. There is also a second pond along the top of the north side slope.

Nearby Parks and Green Spaces:
The Royal Oak Drive Wetlands is located just across the road from the start of this walk.

Royal Oak Ravine

Royal Oak Way Wetlands

Royal Oak Way and Rocky Ridge Road intersection
Bus: 426
Bird Watching, Rest Area

Description:
This small wetlands is located beside an ornamental park area on Royal Oak Way. There are benches for anyone wanting to just sit and relax. Waterfowl have been observed on several visits to this area. There is no path around the outside edge of the wetlands.

Sherwood Pathway

Sherwood Way NW
Bus: No regular service
Walking

Description:
This new district is still being developed. At the present time there are some walking paths. From Sherwood Way a path leads around the south side of the district. There is also a path heading north from Sherwood Way past a small pond. As the district continues to develop these paths will likely be extended.

Area Three

The boundaries of this area are Shaganappi Trail on the west, John Laurie Boulevard and McKnight Boulevard on the south, Deerfoot Trail on the east and the city limits on the north. The districts in this area are Beddington, Country Hills, Coventry Hills, Evanston, Harvest Hills, Hidden Valley, Huntington Hills, Kincora, MacEwan, North Haven, Panorama Hills, Sandstone and Thorncliffe.

"Either go far into the wilderness where none has been, or else find some undiscovered place under everybody's nose."
- Aldo Leopold

Hanson Ranch Wetlands

North Calgary Parks and Green Spaces - Area Three

Area Three Map

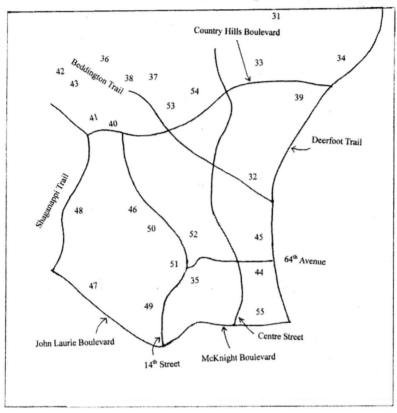

31. Barker Memorial Park
32. Confluence Park
33. Country Hills Pond
34. Coventry Hills Pathway
35. Egerts Park
36. Evanston Pond
37. Hanson Ranch Escarpment
38. Hanson Ranch Wetlands
39. Harvest Hills Lake
40. Hidden Valley Lake
41. Hidden Valley Pathway
42. Kincora Pathway
43. Kincora Pond
44. Laycock Park
45. Nose Creek - McKnight to Confluence Park
46. Nose Hill - Aspen Grove
47. Many Owls Valley
48. Meadowlark Prairie
49. Mule Deer Plateau
50. Porcupine Valley
51. Rubbing Stone Hill
52. Nose Hill Springs Park
53. Panorama Hills Escarp.
54. Panorama Hills Pathway
55. Thorncliffe Community

Barker Memorial Park

Covemeadow Road NE
Bus: No regular service
Historic Plaques, Playground

Description:

This small community park is one of several parks in Calgary that pay tribute to early homesteaders. Barker Memorial Park is in memory of Jack and Elizabeth Barker. The four plaques in the park were erected by the Nose Creek Historical Society.

Barker Memorial Park on the site of the Jack and Elizabeth Barker homestead

History:

As you stand in this park surrounded by the residences of this new district, try to imagine what the area might have been like when Jack Barker rode the train from Ontario to Calgary in 1889. In July of 1893, he built his homestead in the area where this park is located. He married Elizabeth Adams in 1899 and

60

together they raised eleven children. The family donated land about 400 metres west of this park for a school, a church and a community hall. Beddington School was the school for children in this area from 1902 to 1945. Beddington United Church was used from 1913 to 1968. Beddington Community Hall was used from 1922 to 1990. On the Calgary-Edmonton railway line there was a siding called Beddington, named after a location in Surrey, England.

Hopefully during the next few years there might be more parks named for early Calgary area homesteaders.

Confluence Park

Beddington Trail and Beddington Boulevard NE
Bus: 46/146, 86, 88
Cycling, Natural Area, Walking

West Nose Creek valley in Confluence Park

Description:
West Nose Creek joins Nose Creek at the east end of

this natural park. This long thin park is located on the north side of Beddington Trail. The paved path through the park is an extension of the Nose Creek Pathway. You have several route options as the path splits several times. At the main parking lot on Beddington Trail there is a washroom building and a few picnic tables.

There is a second parking lot at the south end of Harvest Hills Boulevard next to a golf driving range. One of the more interesting features in the park is a large glacial erratic known locally as *"Split Rock"*. The erratic is a short walk from the Harvest Hills Boulevard parking lot. You can follow the path west of Harvest Hills Boulevard although there is more traffic noise.

Split Rock in Confluence Park

Nearby Parks and Green Spaces:
From the east end of Confluence Park the Nose Creek Pathway can be followed south.

Country Hills Pond

Country Village Road and Country Village Link
Bus: 86
Bird Watching, Cycling, Playground, Walking

Description:
This large pond is located just north of Country Hills Town Centre. At the time of writing, townhouses and condominiums were still being constructed around the perimeter of the pond. Cardel Place, a large recreation complex with arenas, pool, gymnasium and library, is adjacent to the northwest corner of the pond.

Pond view looking north

Waterfowl are often attracted to the pond in large numbers. A paved path around the pond makes for a very enjoyable walk or bike ride. There is a gazebo at the south end of the pond next to the shopping centre.

Coventry Hills Pathway

Covington Road NE
Bus: 86
Cycling, Walking

Description:
This path is located along the east side of the district. The south end of the path overlooks Nose Creek and the railway line to Edmonton. As the path nears its north end beside Coverton Heights it passes along the edge of a dry pond. There is also a path leading off the main path into the district.

Looking north along the Coventry Hills Pathway

Egerts Park

Norfolk Drive and Norfolk Way NW
Bus: 4/5, 20
Ball Diamond, Playground, Soccer Field, Views, Walking

Description:

This large community park in Upper North Haven has the rough shape of an upside down Y. There is an excellent view from the elevated west side of the park.

You can follow the paved path at the north end of the park across Norfolk Drive and through a green space to a tunnel under 14th Street. The tunnel leads to Nose Hill Park just south of 64th Avenue beside the Rubbing Stone Hill parking lot.

A second paved path leads southeast through the park to Northmount Drive just south of Thorneycroft Drive. The third paved path leads south in the park to the corner where John Laurie Boulevard joins McKnight Boulevard.

View looking south towards downtown Calgary

Nearby Parks and Green Spaces:

The Rubbing Stone Hill area of Nose Hill Park is the closest park or green space to Egerts Park.

Evanston Pond

Evansmeade Circle
Bus: No regular service
Bird Watching

Description:
   This small pond area is located near the entrance to the district. Bird watchers might consider bringing their binoculars and spending some time sitting on one of the benches at the gazebo which is located overlooking the pond.

Gazebo overlooking Evanston Pond

Hanson Ranch Escarpment

Hidden Creek Drive and Hidden Creek Boulevard NW
Bus: No regular service
Playground, Sculpture, Views, Walking

Description:
    As you enter the district of Hanson Ranch you are heading towards a large escarpment slope. At the base of the slope is a playground. Look for the sculptures of a man riding his horse followed by his dog. The developer, Hopewell, placed the sculptures here in 1999.
    Several trails head up the escarpment from the playground if visitors are interested in climbing higher to enjoy the view.

Playground and Sculpture at Hanson Ranch Escarpment

History:
    A plaque near the playground recognizes that the district was named as a tribute to Gene and Sally Hanson and their family who for 54 years ranched the land where the district is located.

Nearby Parks and Green Spaces:
    Hanson Ranch Wetlands is a short walk from the playground. From the top of the escarpment a trail leads south a short distance to the Panorama Hills

Escarpment.

Hanson Ranch Wetlands

Hidden Creek Drive NW
Bus: No regular service
Bird Watching, Walking

Hanson Ranch Wetlands

Description:
This wetlands area along West Nose Creek is on both sides of Hidden Creek Drive as you enter the district of Hanson Ranch. It is an enjoyable walk along the paved path. With luck, visitors might see one or more kinds of waterfowl and shore birds.

Nearby Parks and Green Spaces:
This wetlands is just a short walk from the Hanson Ranch Escarpment.

Harvest Hills Lake

Harvest Lake Drive NE
Bus: 88
Ball Diamonds, Bird Watching, Picnic Tables, Playground,
Soccer Fields, Walking

View looking north

Description:

Waterfowl are attracted to this man-made lake in large numbers. There is a parking lot and a large grass area at the south end of the lake on Harvest Lake Drive. From the parking lot a path leads around the outside edge of the lake behind the houses. From the parking lot it is a short walk to the west to ball diamonds and soccer fields which adjoin the school field of Ascension of Our Lord School. There is a playground by the school.

At the north end of the lake near where Harvest Wood Road joins Harvest Hills Drive there is a path between houses, leading to the lake. There is a playground by this path.

Hidden Valley Lake

Hidden Valley Drive and 200 Hidden Valley Landing NW
Bus: 118
Bird Watching, Playground, Walking

Geese on Hidden Valley Lake

Description:
    This man-made lake is smaller than some of the other lakes or ponds in this area. However it is very popular with the waterfowl. There is no path around the outside edge so visitors will have to walk on the grass behind the houses that back onto the lake. There is a small playground at the south end of the lake beside the end of Hidden Valley Heights. There is also an access point to the lake between houses near the north end of Hidden Valley Heights.

Hidden Valley Pathway

Hidden Valley Drive and Hidden Green NW
Bus: 118
Cycling, Walking

View of ravine looking north

Description:
From the starting location on Hidden Valley Drive this path can be followed north or south. On the north side of Hidden Valley Drive the path drops down into a dry pond area and soon turns to head in a southeasterly direction along the base of a slope located on the right side of the path.

On the south side of Hidden Valley Drive the path passes along the top of a small escarpment overlooking a ravine.

Nearby Parks and Green Spaces:
When the path reaches the end of the ravine it goes through a tunnel under Country Hills Boulevard and into the district of MacEwan. The path then cuts across a

corner of MacEwan and goes through a second tunnel under Shaganappi Trail and into the district of Edgemont. From there the path can be followed to the Edgemont Ravines Path.

Kincora Pathway

Kincora Drive and Kincora Boulevard NW
Bus: No regular service
Cycling, Walking

Pathway in Kincora

Description:
This new district is still being developed. The pathway starts on the west side of Kincora Drive just south of Kincora Boulevard. The path soon splits. Both branches follow shallow ravines through the district. As this district continues to develop the pathway system may be extended. A loop walk could be done by following one of the two branches of the path until reaching Kincora Drive. By following Kincora Drive it is possible to reach

72

the second branch of the path and follow it back to the starting point.

Nearby Parks and Green Spaces:
Kincora Pond is just a short distance along Kincora Drive from the start of the pathway.

Kincora Pond

Kincora Drive and Kincora Landing NW
Bus: No regular service
Bird Watching, Views

View of Kincora pond looking south

Description:
There are several information plaques beside the path leading to this small pond. The plaques include information on the origin of the community name and a map of the community.

One plaque has details about the pond which was constructed as a storm water management site with the

73

features of a natural wetland.

Nearby Parks and Green Spaces:
Kincora Pathway starts just a short distance from this pond.

Laycock Park
North on 6th Street NE from Beaver Dam Road
Bus: 4/5, 32
Ball Diamond, Cycling, Playground, Walking, Washrooms

Nose Creek flows through the park

Description:
This is one of the parks built along the Nose Creek Pathway. Users of the pathway may want to stop here for a rest or families on a cycling excursion may want to give the children a break at the playground. Some visitors may be interested in exploring along the edge of Nose Creek.

History:
The park is named for Thomas and Martha Laycock. The couple moved to Calgary from England in 1886 and established their family farm in the area now occupied by the park.

Nearby Parks and Green Spaces:
From the south end of the park the Nose Creek Pathway can be followed as far as its junction with the Bow River Pathway. Heading north from the park, the pathway can be followed north of 64th Avenue to the pathway in Confluence Park.

Nose Creek Pathway - McKnight Boulevard to Confluence Park

Blackthorn Road NE
Bus: 4/5, 32
Cycling, Walking

Description:
The suggested starting location is on Blackthorn Road overlooking Laycock Park. Walk down the paved path into the park. From Laycock Park south to McKnight Boulevard the Nose Creek Pathway passes through a narrow green space before going behind a small shopping centre and passing under McKnight Boulevard. There is an industrial area on the east side of the creek.

The route north from Laycock Park is more pleasant than the path heading south. The path passes under 64th Avenue and then enters a green space. On the right are the railway tracks, Nose Creek and Deerfoot Trail. On the left there are residences at the top of an escarpment slope.

Nearby Parks and Green Spaces:
The Nose Creek Pathway continues south of McKnight Boulevard to the Bow River. The Nose Creek Pathway heading north passes under Beddington Trail and joins

the Confluence Park path.

Path leading to Nose Creek Pathway north of 64th Avenue

Nose Hill Park - Aspen Grove
MacEwan Glen Drive and MacEwan Park View NW
Bus: 46
Cycling, Natural Area, Views, Walking

Description:
This area is at the north end of Nose Hill Park adjacent to the communities of MacEwan, Sandstone and Beddington. Much of this area is composed of north facing slopes with stands of aspen.

There is a large interpretive sign at the starting point. From here visitors can follow one of the trails up the hill. An alternate route is to follow the trail leading along the bottom of a ravine that extends in a southwesterly direction from the starting point. This trail passes a small pond. The trail can be followed up the ravine to the top of the hill just east of the parking lot for the Meadowlark

Prairie area of the park.

Nearby Parks and Green Spaces:
This area of Nose Hill Park is closest to the Meadowlark Prairie and Porcupine Valley areas of the park.

Ravine in Aspen Grove area of Nose Hill Park

Nose Hill Park - Many Owls Valley

John Laurie Boulevard and Brisebois Drive NW
Bus: 43/143, 22/122
Cycling, Historic Plaque, Natural Area, Views, Walking

Description:
This area of the park is along the park's south boundary beside John Laurie Boulevard. There is a parking lot at this site. The city has constructed a pedestrian overpass across John Laurie connecting the

park to the John Laurie Pathway on the south side. This overpass makes access to the park much easier from the districts on the south side of John Laurie Boulevard.

From the parking lot visitors have a choice of several trails leading up the hill.

Many Owls area of Nose Hill Park

History:

On the south side of the parking lot, a plaque honoring John Laurie (1899-1959) is affixed to a large rock. A high school teacher in Calgary, he played a huge role in the encouragement and development of a better understanding between First Nations and non-First Nations people. The rock was a gift from the Stoney Nation at Morley.

Nearby Parks and Green Spaces:

The John Laurie Pathway is just across the overpass from the parking lot.

Nose Hill Park - Meadowlark Prairie

Shaganappi Trail and Edgemont Boulevard NW
Bus: 77
Cycling, Natural Area, Views, Walking, Washrooms

Trail heading east in Meadowlark Prairie
area of Nose Hill Park

Description:
    The parking lot for this area of the park can be accessed from the above named intersection. At the present time this is the only parking lot within the park that has washrooms. For park visitors not wanting to face the steep climb up the hill this is a good location to start a visit to the park. The trails and the paved path leading into the park from this parking lot start at the top of the hill.
    Visitors have several route choices from the parking lot. A line of power poles can be followed east across the park to where there is an excellent view at the top of the

escarpment overlooking 14th Street. Near the beginning of this route the trail passes through the top end of the ravine that leads down to the Aspen Grove starting point.

There is a paved interpretive trail that can be followed from the parking lot. As well there are numerous other trails leading off into the distance across the park. Some of these trails might be closed if proposed changes are made to the park.

Nearby Parks and Green Spaces:
This area of the park is closest to the Aspen Grove area of the park.

Nose Hill Park - Mule Deer Plateau
14th Street just south of North Haven Drive NW
Bus: 4/5
Cycling, Natural Area, Views, Walking

Description:
To access this area of the park visitors follow an old gravel pit road into the park from 14th Street. Visitors can park along the edge of the road or continue to a small parking lot at the end of the road. This parking lot overlooks 14th Street. From this location there is an excellent view east across the city or south towards downtown. If the section of the old road that is fenced off to vehicles is followed to the top of the hill it leads into an old gravel pit area.

Anyone traveling to the Mule Deer Plateau area of the park by bus needs to exit the bus near the intersection of North Haven Drive and Ninga Road. From there head west along Ninga Road to a small green space. Walk through this green space to where a tunnel under 14th Street leads into Nose Hill Park just to the north of the old gravel pit road.

This starting point for exploring the park also has a shorter climb to the top of the hill than from most of the other starting locations.

A ravine leading north from the John Laurie Boulevard side of the park can be reached if visitors walk west from the starting location and try to follow a route close to the top edge of the slope. This ravine is much narrower than the ravine in Porcupine Valley.

View of downtown Calgary from Mule Deer Plateau area of Nose Hill Park

The bottom end of this ravine can be reached by entering the park at the southeast corner by 14th Street and John Laurie Boulevard. From this corner, walk west along the bottom edge of the slope until the ravine is reached. Parking is very limited when starting from the southeast corner of the park.

Nearby Parks and Green Spaces:
This area of the park is closest to the Porcupine Valley area of the park.

Nose Hill Park - Porcupine Valley

14th Street and Berkley Gate NW
Bus: 46
Cycling, Natural Area, Views, Walking

Trail in Porcupine Valley area of Nose Hill Park

Description:

Visitors can follow a paved path to reach the main paved path in this area. This path extends up the hill along the north side of the valley. The path ends at the top of the hill. Going east this path leaves Nose Hill Park through a tunnel under 14th Street and passes through a green space between Beddington and Huntington Hills districts. There are also trails leading up the hill on both sides of the valley path. Please note that these trails on both sides of the valley are some of the steeper trails within the park.

Nearby Parks and Green Spaces:
This area of the park is between Rubbing Stone Hill and Aspen Grove.

On the north side of Porcupine Valley

Nose Hill Park - Rubbing Stone Hill

14th Street and 64th Avenue NW
Bus: 2, 4/5
Cycling, Natural Area, Views, Walking

Description:
From the parking lot the main feature of this area is a large glacial erratic which can be seen higher up the hill. An old road can be followed to the erratic. If this old road is followed to the top of the hill it leads into an old gravel pit area. There are also other trails fanning out from the parking lot.

On the south side of the lot is a plaque on a rock

dated 1992. The plaque recognizes the contributions of both the provincial and municipal governments and the efforts of a group of Calgary citizens who had the vision to propose the creation of Nose Hill Park. The dedication and persistence of these citizens in achieving their goal has provided Calgarians and visitors to the city with this large natural park within the boundaries of the city. The area occupied by Nose Hill Park could have become a residential district.

Rubbing Stone Hill area of Nose Hill Park

Nearby Parks and Green Spaces:
Just south of the parking lot a trail leads into the park through a tunnel under 14th Street. This trail leads to Egerts Park. This area of the park is between Porcupine Valley and Mule Deer Plateau on the 14th Street side of the park.

Nose Hill Spring Park

7th Street and 75th Avenue NW
Bus: 2
Historic Plaque

Description:

This tiny community park is located in Huntington Hills adjacent to the east fence of the Dr. J.K. Mulloy School field. A small spring of water surfaces in the park before seeping underground. A plaque in the park indicates that explorer David Thompson may have stopped at this location. The plaque also mentions that First Nations people traveling through the area probably also made use of this spring.

Nose Hill Spring Park

Panorama Hills Escarpment

Panorama Hills Landing
Bus: No regular service
Cycling, Views, Walking

Description:
There is a tremendous view from the pathway on the top of this escarpment overlooking the West Nose Creek Valley. Parking for anyone living outside the district is restricted. One location to park is near the west end of Panorama Hills Landing beside a small park. From here a path leads between houses and then across Panorama Hills Heights and between more houses to reach the path along the top of the escarpment.

View looking north towards Hanson Ranch

Just north of this location the path turns and heads east. The path leading south along the top of the escarpment goes past some very interesting rock outcroppings. The path also passes through a ravine before entering a fenced off section within the lands of

The Ridge of Country Hills Golf Club. At the south end of the path, there is no parking along Country Hills Boulevard.

Nearby Parks and Green Spaces:
At the time of writing a dirt trail leads north from the paved path along the top of the escarpment to the top of the Hanson Ranch Escarpment.

Panorama Hills Pathway
Panatella Boulevard and Panatella Close NW
Bus: No regular service
Walking

Panorama Hills Pathway

Description:
On the south side of Panatella Boulevard a path leads south through an open area between houses. There is a small creek flowing through this area. The path ends beside a pond near the intersection of Panamount

87

Boulevard and Harvest Hills Boulevard. The district is still being developed on the north side of Panatella Boulevard. At the time of writing a small pond and more pathways were being developed.

Description:
    On the south side of Panatella Boulevard a path leads south through an open area between houses. There is a small creek flowing through this area. The path ends beside a pond near the intersection of Panamount Boulevard and Harvest Hills Boulevard. The district is still being developed on the north side of Panatella Boulevard. At the time of writing a small pond and more pathways were being developed.

Thorncliffe Community Park
56th Avenue and Centre Street NW
Bus: 3
Arena, Ball Diamond, Community Hall, Playground, Soccer Field, Tobogganing

Description:
    There is a shallow ravine extending south from 56th Avenue south to McKnight Boulevard. The open slopes on both sides of the ravine can be used for tobogganing. The community hall and arena are located on the west side of the ravine. On the north side of 56th Avenue there is a playground, ball diamond and soccer field.

Area Four

The boundaries for this area are Crowchild Trail and Shaganappi Trail on the west, John Laurie Boulevard and McKnight Boulevard on the north, Deerfoot Trail on the east and the Bow River on the south. The area includes the districts of Banff Trail, Brentwood, Briar Hill, Bridgeland, Cambrian Heights, Capitol Hill, Charleswood, Collingwood, Crescent Heights, Greenview, Highland Park, Highwood, Hillhurst, Mount Pleasant, Mountview, Renfrew, Rosemont, Sunnyside, Tuxedo, West Hillhurst and Winston Heights

"Citizens are apparently acquiring the park habit in a marked degree, whole families during the hot weather seeming to almost reside in them."
- William Reader, Superintendent of Calgary Parks, 1917

View towards Fort Calgary from Centenary Park

Area Four Map

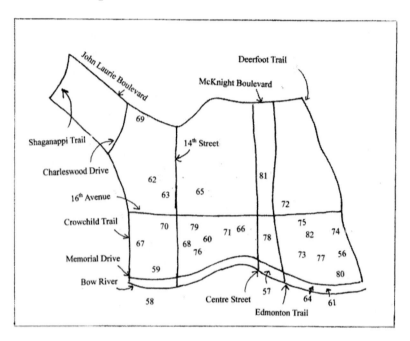

56. Bottomlands Park	69. John Laurie Pathway
57. Bow River - Centre Street to Nose Creek	70. Lions Park
	71. McHugh Bluff
58. Bow River - Crowchild to Centre Street	72. Munro Park
	73. Murdoch Park
59. Broadview Park	74. Nose Creek - Bow River to McKnight
60. Burns Memorial Gardens	
	75. Renfrew Athletic Park
61. Calgary Zoo	76. Riley Park
62. Canmore Park	77. Riverside Park
63. Capitol Hill Community	78. Rotary Park
64. Centenary Park	79. SAIT - Martin Cohos Commons
65. Confederation Park	
66. Crescent Park	80. Tom Campbell's Hill
67. Grand Trunk Park	81. Tuxedo Community
68. Hillhurst Sunnyside Community	82. Ukrainian Pioneers Park

Bottomlands Park

St Georges Drive NE
Bus: 19
Picnic Tables, Playground, Rest Area, Washrooms
(seasonal)

Description:
This small park is located along the Nose Creek
Pathway between Memorial Drive and 7th Avenue NE. The
park could be used as a rest area for anyone cycling, in-
line skating or walking along the Nose Creek Pathway.
Families cycling along the pathway might want to stop at
this park so the children can spend a few minutes at the
playground.

Bottomlands Park

Nearby Parks and Green Spaces:
Tom Campbell's Hill Park is a short walk from this

91

location.

Bow River Pathway - Centre Street to Nose Creek

Calgary Zoo - West Parking Lot (south end of Baines Bridge)
Bus: Bridgeland C-Train Station
Bird Watching, Cycling, In-Line Skating, Walking

Description:
The suggested starting point for this section of pathway is to use the west parking lot for the zoo, which is located at the south end of the Baines Bridge. The pathway is on the north side of this bridge.

Heading east the pathway soon enters a narrow area between the zoo fence and the river. You may be able to spot some of the zoo animals through the fence. At the confluence of the Bow River and Nose Creek there is a pleasant little rest area with benches and an information plaque. The plaque mentions when the Nose Creek valley was a Calgary red-light district. Several kinds of birds or waterfowl can usually be observed in this area.

The large black structure of the CPR bridge for northbound trains is located close by. Pearce Estate Park is across the river on the east side of the train bridge. This park will be included in the southeast parks and green spaces book.

The path leading west from the Baines Bridge soon splits in two to separate the walkers and runners from cyclists. After passing the Bridgeland C-Train Station the green space between Memorial Drive and the river becomes a bit wider. As the path nears Edmonton Trail area it goes under four bridges. From Edmonton Trail to Centre Street Bridge the pathway follows a narrow green space. The underpasses on the pathway for the Edmonton Trail bridges and the Centre Street Bridge may be closed from time to time if the river is high or if there is a build up of river ice in the winter.

History:
Following the pathway from east to west, the first bridge at the Edmonton Trail area is the Harry Kroeger C-Train Bridge, closely followed by the north-bound Langevin Bridge which opened in 1972. The third bridge is the older south-bound Langevin Bridge which was constructed in 1910 replacing a wooden bridge that was built in 1888. The final bridge in this area is the 4th Avenue Flyover.

Pathway users may want to take along a copy of Harry Sanders' book *Historic Walks of Calgary,* as there are several historic buildings in the nearby Bridgeland-Riverside area on the north side of Memorial Drive.

Rest area at the confluence of
Nose Creek with Bow River

Nearby Parks and Green Spaces:
From the rest area at the confluence of the Bow River and Nose Creek, pathway users can choose to head north along the Nose Creek Pathway. The other pathway options are to continue east along the Bow River Pathway or to cross an overpass above Deerfoot Trail to reach the start of the Irrigation Canal Pathway. These two pathway routes will also be in the southeast parks and green spaces book.

Centenary Park and the Calgary Zoo are both adjacent to the west zoo parking lot. Tom Campbell's Hill Park is also a short distance away on the north side of Memorial Drive. These three parks are all included in the parks and green spaces for area four. At Centre Street, the pathway continues west.

The Bow River Pathway east of Centre Street on the other side of the river will be in the southeast parks and green spaces book.

Bow River Pathway - Crowchild Trail to Centre Street
Memorial Drive and 10th Street NW
Bus: 1, 4/5, 9
Cycling, Information Centre, Picnic Tables, Programs, Walking, Washrooms

Description:
The suggested starting point for this section of pathway is at the parking lot beside the Calgary Outdoor Resource Centre. This parking lot just west of 10th Street is only accessible to eastbound traffic on Memorial Drive. There is a charge for parking in this lot. The centre has brochures on parks and recreation programs, pathway maps and a variety of books for sale. The washrooms in the centre are available to the public when the resource centre is open. On the south side of the building overlooking the river is a lovely rest area with benches

and picnic tables.

Most of the pathway between the fire hall and 14th Street Bridge is twinned. The green space here is wider than other sections along the pathway. There is another short section of twinned pathway west of the 14th Street Bridge. The green space from 14th Street to Crowchild Trail is very narrow in sections.

On the east side of Hillhurst Louise Bridge there is a very congested section of pathway until it passes the C-Train Bridge. East of the train bridge, the pathway is twinned as it passes through a wider green space. After the Prince's Island pedestrian bridge, the green space again narrows and there is only one path. This section of pathway gets a lot of use - whether it is weekend walkers, runners or cyclists; people walking or cycling to and from work downtown; or the downtown workers out for a noon time walk or run.

Hillhurst Louise Bridge

History:

The Calgary Parks Outdoor Resource Centre is located on the main floor of the old fire hall No. 6 which was constructed in 1910. The building was used as a fire hall until 1964. The fire hall was renovated by the city in 2002. Just east of the fire hall is Hillhurst (Louise) Bridge. There is a historic plaque nearby. The first bridge crossing in this area was the Bow Marsh Bridge, a wooden structure used from 1888 to 1906. A steel bridge was then used from 1906 to 1927. This bridge was known as the Louise Bridge. The present day bridge constructed in 1920-21 was named the Hillhurst Bridge although the name Louise was still used. Today the name of the bridge is Hillhurst Louise Bridge.

Calgary Parks Outdoor Resource Centre

At Centre Street, the first river crossing was Fogg's Ferry. A steel truss bridge then replaced the ferry. It was privately built and operated as a toll bridge. The city purchased the bridge in 1911 and it was used for four more years before being condemned. The north approach of this bridge was washed away in a 1915 flood. The present day bridge, with the lion and buffalo head sculptures, opened in 1916. James L. Thomson was the sculptor of the lions. One of the original lions can be viewed in front of the Municipal Building at 8th Avenue and Macleod Trail SE

Pathway users may want to take along a copy of Harry Sanders' book *Historic Walks of Calgary,* as there are several historic buildings near the fire hall.

Nearby Parks and Green Spaces:
Prince's Island Park and the Bow River Pathway on the other side of the river will be described in the southwest parks and green spaces book.

This section of Bow River Pathway connects with the pathway west of Crowchild Trail and the pathway east of Centre Street.

Broadview Park
Broadview Road and 20th Street NW
Bus: 1
Soccer

Description:
Soccer has been played in this park since the 1950s. The park is located beside Memorial Drive. The field is used by adult soccer players. Soccer fans might enjoy a visit here on a warm summer evening to watch a game under the floodlights.

Nearby Parks and Green Spaces:
The Bow River Pathway from Crowchild Trail to Centre Street is across Memorial Drive from this park.

Burns Memorial Gardens

10th Street and SAIT Way NW
Bus: 4/5, 9
Gardens, Rest Area

Description:
This impressive rock garden is on the escarpment slope on the west side of 10th Street, adjacent to the northeast corner of Riley Park. Visitors can follow a network of paths through the gardens. If you are strolling this park on a summer weekend be careful you don't wander through the midst of a group taking wedding photos. At the south end of the gardens is a floral display depicting Senator Pat Burns' brand.

Walking path through the gardens

History:
The gardens were developed in the 1950s, using sandstone acquired from the demolition of Senator Burns home at 12th Avenue and 4th Street SW. Burns (1856-1937) moved to Calgary from Ontario in 1890. He was a very successful entrepreneur with his business interests

including P. Burns and Company Ltd, which became one of the biggest meat-packing businesses in the country. There is a national historic plaque recognizing Patrick Burns in the gardens. There is also a plaque recognizing Alex Munro in the gardens. He served as Calgary's parks superintendent for 21 years. Munro Park is included in area four.

After strolling through the gardens you may want to head south along 10th Street to visit the coffee shops, restaurants or shops.

Nearby Parks and Green Spaces:
The gardens are adjacent to Riley Park. SAIT is a short walk up the hill from the gardens.

Calgary Zoo
Memorial Drive and St. George's Drive NE
Bus: Zoo C-Train Station
Botanical Gardens, Concessions, Gardens, Picnic Tables, Prehistoric Park, Souvenir Shop, Zoo

Picnic at St. George's Island, Calgary, Alberta, August 1915. (Glenbow Archives NA-1604-73)

Description:

It may require more than one visit to the Calgary Zoo to see everything. If visitors try to view all the animal facilities in one trip there probably won't be time to walk through the Prehistoric Park or to view the Botanical Gardens. There are numerous food outlets and rest areas throughout the park.

History:

At one time there were three separate islands in this area. The islands were called St. George's, St. Andrew's and St. Patrick's. Over the years changes have been made to the landscape and the area is now one large island.

Bandstand, St. George's Island, Calgary. 1942.
(Glenbow Archives NA-1538-3)

Early Calgary residents enjoyed visiting this location. Visitors to the islands used a ferry from 1891 until the building of the first bridge in 1908. A pavilion was constructed in 1912. The Zoo had its beginnings in 1918 when a small enclosure was constructed to showcase two mule deer. Other early facilities in the park included a merry go round and a dance floor. In 1928 the Calgary Zoological Society was formed with Tom Baines being appointed the first keeper. The early version of today's Prehistoric Park was started in 1933.

Nearby Parks and Green Spaces:
Centenary Park is located adjacent to the west parking lot of the Zoo. The Bow River Pathway is on both sides of the river in this area. The north side pathway is described in this book. The south side pathway will be included in the southeast book.

Canmore Park

Canmore Road and 19th Street NW
Bus: 10, 407
Ball Diamond, Children's Wading Pool, Playground, Tennis Courts, Tobogganing, Walking, Washrooms (seasonal)

Description:
Some people may know this park by the name North Capitol Hill. This large community park is located north of Canmore Road, between the districts of Banff Trail and Collingwood. The hilly terrain of the park has made it a popular location for cross country running races. On hot summer days the small wading pool becomes a popular spot for small children and their parents to visit. The hills in the park can be used for tobogganing.

Nearby Parks and Green Spaces:
From the east side of the park along 19th Street a path can be followed from 19th Street to 14th Street along the south side of the Confederation Park Golf Course. At 14th Street the path goes through a tunnel and into

Confederation Park.

View looking west from 19th Street

Capitol Hill Community Park

20th Avenue and 14th Street NW
Bus: 10
Ball Diamond, Community Hall and Playground

Description:
This community park is one city block in size. The park is enclosed with a wire fence and trees or shrubs along the edges. There is a similar sized park in the southwest community of Glengarry.

Some years ago the park was a favorite destination for hockey players who gathered at the outdoor rink for informal games. The boards from this rink have been removed from the park.

History:
The park is one of Calgary's older community parks. The park was developed in the 1930s, with a tree and

shrub border being planted along the four sides of the park. Capitol Hill Cottage School, one of only three remaining cottage schools in Calgary is located on 21st Avenue across the street from the park. There were seventeen two-room cottage schools built between 1910 and 1912 to provide space for the increasing number of students.

Nearby Parks and Green Spaces:
Confederation Park is only a few blocks from this park.

Capitol Hill community hall

Centenary Park
Memorial Drive and Zoo Road NE
C-Train: Bridgeland Memorial Station
Natural Area, Picnic Tables, Walking

Description:
This Bow River island park is located at the west end of the Calgary Zoo adjacent to the zoo parking lot. It is

located on what was once a separate island named St. Patrick's. There were three distinct islands in this area named St. Patrick's, St. George's and St. Andrews. There is now just one large island. The Zoo occupies the other two islands which are collectively known now as St. George's Island. Centenary Park was developed in 1984 as a Calgary Centennial project to commemorate the centennial of Calgary's incorporation as a city. This project was funded by Atco Ltd.

Picnic tables in the park make this a great location for pathway users to stop for a rest or a snack.

Small bridge in park

History:

The Dominion Government donated the three islands to the city for use as park space. The islands were named in 1890. In 1907 the area became a city park. At one time there was a campground on St. Patrick's Island. An old paved road probably used for the campground runs along the north side of the park. For a few years there were some zoo animals kept in enclosures in this park.

Nearby Parks and Green Spaces:
The George King pedestrian bridge at the west end of the park leads across the river to the Bow River Pathway on the south side of the river and to Fort Calgary Park. These areas will be included in the southeast parks and green spaces book. The Bow River Pathway on the north side of the river can be reached by crossing the Tom Baines Bridge beside the parking lot. This pathway is included in area four of this book.

View of downtown from park

Confederation Park

10th Street north of 23rd Avenue NW
Bus: 4/5
Ball Diamond, Bird Watching, City Parks and Recreation Area Office, Community Hall, Cycling, Picnic Tables, Playground, Sculpture, Skating, Tennis Courts, Tobogganing, Walking, Washrooms

Description:
This beautiful jewel in Calgary's park system stretches

from 14th Street and 24th Avenue NW east to 30th Avenue near 6th Street. A group of individuals formed the Centennial Ravine Park Society in 1966 to raise funds for a park. Their efforts were very successful, resulting in the dedication of the park in 1967 to recognize Canada's centennial.

A pedestrian tunnel under 10th Street connects the two main areas of the park. On the west side of 10th Street there is a wetlands area which was extensively renovated in 2005. This is a great spot for watching waterfowl and birds. Adjacent to the community hall is a ball diamond and an area for skating. There is also a toboggan hill near the hall. A small playground overlooks the parking lot. A steel and aluminum sculpture entitled *Transition '67* by artist Enzo DiPalma is located near the parking lot on the west side of 10th Street.

Wetlands area west of 10th Street

On the east side of 10th Street a Centennial symbol-shaped flower bed is planted every summer. There is also a more formal area with the flags of Canada's provinces and territories and a large stone map of Canada. Towards the east end of the park is the City Parks Area Office building with public washrooms. There is also an excellent toboggan hill just east of 10th Street.

Nearby Parks and Green Spaces:
At the west end of the park the path passes through a tunnel under 14th Street. From here the path follows along the south side of the Confederation Park Golf Course and crosses 19th Street into Canmore Park.

Transition '67 sculpture beside 10th Street

Crescent Park

Crescent Road and 2nd Street NW
Bus: 2, 3
Ball Diamond, Community Hall, Gardens, Historic Plaque, Outdoor Rink, Picnic Tables, Playground, Tennis, Washrooms (seasonal)

Description:

This is another of Calgary's older community parks. The south side of the park is the more ornamental section with flower gardens and picnic tables. There is an excellent view towards downtown Calgary from the benches on the south side of the park. Two rows of trees and bushes separate the three areas of the park. In the central portion of the park there are two ball diamonds and a washroom building. The north section of the park has the community hall, tennis courts, playground and outdoor skating rink. There is also a curling club adjacent to this section.

Ornamental section of park

History:

A plaque on the east side of the park indicates this was Calgary's first park on the North Hill. The land was dedicated for park use in the 1920s. The first tree was planted here in 1923. In the 1930s trees and shrubs were planted along the edges of the park.

Nearby Parks and Green Spaces:
McHugh Bluff is just across the road from the park.

Grand Trunk Park

5th Avenue and 23rd Street NW
Bus: 9, 20, 72/73
Historic Building, Playground

Description:
This small community park is located near the west end of West Hillhurst. There is a playground in the park.

Grand Trunk Cottage School

History:
At one time this district was called Grand Trunk. On the west side of the park is Grand Trunk Cottage School, one of three remaining cottage schools in Calgary. The other two buildings are on 21st Avenue NW across from

Capitol Hill Park and on 12th Street NW south of Riley Park.

Hillhurst-Sunnyside Community

12th Street and 5th Avenue NW
Bus: 9, 10
Ball Diamond, Basketball, Community Hall, Soccer Field, Tennis

Description:
This is another of Calgary's older community parks. In the summer months the farmer's market held here every week attracts many buyers. There is also a weekly flea market held in the community hall.

Hillhurst Sunnyside Community Park

History:
This community park has a long history in this

district. In 1914 two skating rinks were developed in the park with one being used for hockey. The park also became very popular for team sports including football. The park facilities included a grandstand for spectators.

St. Barnabas Anglican Church is adjacent to the northeast corner of the park. In 1957, a fire destroyed the church building which was constructed in 1912. The church tower was the only section of this building to survive. The tower was then incorporated into the construction of the present church building which was built in 1957. There is a small graveyard beside the church.

Across 7th Avenue from the church is Hillhurst School built in 1911. It was one of eighteen sandstone schools constructed in Calgary.

Nearby Parks and Green Spaces:
Riley Park is across 12th Street from the community park. On the far side of Riley Park beside 10th Street is Burns Memorial Gardens.

John Laurie Pathway
John Laurie Boulevard and 19th Street NW
Bus: 4/5, 22/122, 43/143
Ball Diamond, Cycling, Playground, Views, Walking

Description:
This long linear park on the south side of John Laurie Boulevard stretches west from 14th Street to Brenner Drive. Houses back onto the south side of the park. A walking path of about 3 km in length extends from one end of the park to the other. The path has several small hills. There are excellent views along the path.

There are two parking lots at 19th Street, just south of John Laurie Boulevard. If you walk the entire path use caution crossing 19th Street, Charleswood Drive and Brisebois Drive.

History:

John Laurie moved to Calgary from Ontario in 1920. He had a long teaching career at Western Canada College and Crescent Heights High School from 1923 to 1956. He also dedicated himself to the task of improving the life of Alberta's First Nations. There is a plaque honoring Laurie in the Nose Hill Park parking lot at Brisebois Drive and John Laurie Boulevard.

Nearby Parks and Green Spaces:

Just east of Brisebois Drive there is an overpass that opened in 2005 and allows park users to cross over John Laurie Boulevard into the Many Owls Valley area of Nose Hill Park.

John Laurie overpass to Nose Hill Park

Lions Park

19th Street and 14th Avenue NW
Bus: 19, 40, 407
C-Train: Lions Park Station
Playground, Rest Area, Walking

Description:

Most Calgarians associate the name Lions Park with the C-Train Station across from the North Hill Centre. However on the south side of the tracks is a thin park stretching from 19th Street east to 14th Street. This park was developed in 1953 but was reduced in size when the NW C-Train line was built in the 1980s.

There is a playground towards the east end of the green space.

Pathway near Lions Park C-Train Station

McHugh Bluff

Crescent Road and 2nd Street NW
Bus: 2, 3
Historic Plaque, Views, Walking

Description:

This escarpment is along the south side of Crescent Heights and Rosedale. It extends from Centre Street west to 10th Street. A walk along the top of the escarpment beside Crescent Road offers great views south towards downtown and to the southwest. This route has a variety of walking surfaces ranging from dirt trail to paved path. A paved path at the east end of the escarpment leads down to Centre Street opposite the stairs leading up to Rotary Park. At 1st Street a paved path leads down into Sunnyside. At 2nd Street a long set of stairs also leads down into Sunnyside.

View of McHugh Bluff looking east

There is also a paved path known as the Sunnyside Pathway which starts at the base of the escarpment on

3rd Avenue just east of 6th Street. This route can be followed to the bottom of the stairs leading down from Crescent Road. At the west end of the bluff the slope can be climbed from a set of stairs on the north end of 9A Street beside the C-Train tracks. There are other trails on the escarpment but park visitors are encouraged to stay on the main routes if possible.

History:
There is a plaque recognizing Felix McHugh near the top of the stairs at 2nd Street and Crescent Road. He came to Calgary from Ontario in 1883 and homesteaded at the base of the escarpment in what is now the district of Sunnyside.

Sunnyside pathway near bottom of McHugh Bluff

Nearby Parks and Green Spaces:
Crescent Park is across the road from McHugh Bluff at 2nd Street. At the west end of the bluff Burns Memorial

Gardens and Riley Park are a short distance away. At the east end of the bluff Rotary Park is on the other side of Centre Street.

Munro Park

Edmonton Trail and 18th Avenue NE
Bus: 4/5
Ball Diamond, Playground, Soccer Field

Description:
The decorative area at the west end of this community park was named in 1960 for Alex Munro, who served the city of Calgary as parks superintendent for 21 years. There is a plaque in Burns Memorial Gardens to recognize Mr. Munro's contribution to Calgary's parks system.

Alex Munro Park in winter

Murdoch Park

Centre Avenue and 8th Street NE
Bus: 9
Commemorative Wall, Community Hall, Soccer Field

Description:

This new community park has been developed as part of the Bridges redevelopment on the former site of the Calgary General Hospital in Bridgeland. At the west end of the park is a wall that incorporates some of the bricks from the former hospital.

History:

The park is named for George Murdoch who arrived in Calgary in 1883. When Calgary was incorporated as a town in 1884, he was elected as the first mayor.

As the new development in this district continues there are plans for several more parks.

View of St. Matthew's Lutheran Church

On the west side of the park is St. Matthew's Lutheran Church with its prominent steeple. This church was constructed in 1913. There are several other historic buildings within a few blocks of the park. These buildings are described in Harry Sanders' book *Historic Walks of Calgary.*

Nose Creek Pathway - Bow River to McKnight Boulevard

St Georges Drive
Bus: 19
Cycling, In-Line Skating, Walking

Description:
There is a parking lot at the north end of St. Georges Drive just below the 7th Avenue overpass. From here the Nose Creek Pathway can be followed south through Bottomlands Park to where it joins the Bow River Pathway just below the Memorial Drive overpasses. There is a historic plaque that is located in a rest area with benches where Nose Creek flows into the Bow River.

The most pleasant area of this pathway is between the parking lot and the 16th Avenue overpass. In this area the railway tracks, Nose Creek and Deerfoot Trail are on the right. On the left is the escarpment slope leading up to Renfrew. North of 16th Avenue the path enters a fenced off area between two golf courses. From 32nd Avenue north to McKnight Boulevard the path passes through green space that is close to roads with a fair amount of traffic. Nose Creek Memorial Forest is located along this section of pathway.

Nearby Parks and Green Spaces:
The Nose Hill Pathway continues north of McKnight Boulevard. The south end of this pathway connects with the Bow River pathway near the confluence of the Bow River and Nose Creek. Tom Campbell's Hill Park and the

Calgary Zoo are both located close to the south end of this path.

Looking north on the pathway just south of 16th Avenue

Renfrew Athletic Park

13th Avenue and 7th Street NE
Bus: 17,19
Arenas, Ball Diamonds, Indoor Pool, Playground, Soccer Fields, Tennis Courts

Description:
The first facilities in this park were built in the 1950s. The twin arenas are named for Henry Viney and Stew Hendry. Henry Viney was a well-known Calgary sportscaster. He was a strong supporter of minor sports. Stew Hendry was an active supporter of hockey in Calgary for many years. On the north side of the arenas is Ed Corbett Park. Ed Corbett was a staunch supporter of fastball in Calgary. It seems fitting that these three individuals who played an important part in the Calgary

119

sports scene can be honored in the same athletic park.

Riley Park

12th Street and 8th Avenue NW
Bus: 4/5, 9, 10
Cricket, Flower Gardens, Picnic Tables, Playground, Wading Pool, Washrooms

Description:
There are probably few locations in Calgary that are as pleasant as Riley Park on a hot summer day. The park has a beautiful setting with large mature trees and a grass surface that is well maintained by parks staff. Parents with young children can spend some time at the wading pool. On the east side of the park you can walk through the flower gardens. Other visitors may just relax under the shade of a large tree and enjoy the easy-going pace of a cricket game. There are open grassy areas for impromptu ball games.

Flower gardens in Riley Park

On the south and west sides of the park are old ornamental gates. These gates are left over from an era when park visitors could drive into the park at the south gate and circle around most of the perimeter of the park and exit by the west gate. This old road is still in the park.

This park is a suggested finishing spot for those who have spent time shopping along 10th Street and Kensington Road.

Women playing cricket at Riley Park, Calgary, 1921.
(Glenbow Archives NA-2393-1)

History:

In 1910 Ezra Riley donated 20 acres of land for use as a park. Trees and shrubs were planted in the first few years. In 1914 a toboggan slide was constructed on the escarpment to the north of the park. For some years the NWMP flag pole from Fort Calgary was located in the park. The first cricket pitches were developed in 1919. Since that time the park has been Calgary's home of cricket. At one time cricket was also played at Hillhurst, South Calgary and Elbow Park. In the 1920s there was also an old war cannon in the park.

St. Barnabas Anglican Church and Hillhurst School are two historic buildings located on the west side of 12th Street. These buildings are mentioned in the description of Hillhurst Sunnyside Community Park in this section.

Nearby Parks and Green Spaces:
Burns Memorial Gardens are adjacent to the northeast corner of the park. McHugh Bluff is on the east side of 10th Street. SAIT is a short walk up the escarpment on the north side of the park.

Riverside Park
McDougall Road and 11th Street NE
Bus: 9
Ball Diamond, Playground, Rest Area

Description:
This small community park is located adjacent to several seniors residences. There are benches to relax on.

Nearby Parks and Green Spaces:
Murdoch Park is a short walk from this park.

Rotary Park
Centre Street and 7th Avenue NE
Bus: 2, 3
Interpretive Plaques, Picnic Tables, Playground, Private Tennis Club, View, Wading Pool, Washrooms (Seasonal)

Description:
This older city park is located in Crescent Heights. A set of stairs at Centre Street and Samis Road NE leads up to the park.

At the northwest corner of the park on 7th Avenue a

sandstone archway has been placed in recognition of the park rejuvenation that took place in 2001. Along the top of the escarpment at the south end of the park (known as Jim Fish Ridge), a set of plaques have historical information about the city.

Park visitors in the warmer weather might include children and their parents coming to make use of the small wading pool.

The southwest corner of the park is a great location to sit and relax while looking at the view of downtown Calgary and the Prince's Island area. This area is also very popular with local dog walkers.

Wading Pool in Rotary Park

History:

This park was developed in the 1930s. The early facilities included a wading pool and space to play baseball, football and hockey. In the early years the park was known as Mount Pleasant Rotary Park. The private tennis club, Mount Pleasant Tennis Club, located in the park has retained this name even though the Calgary district of Mount Pleasant is a few kilometers from this park.

Nearby Parks and Green Spaces:
McHugh Bluff on the west side of Centre Street is close to this park.

SAIT - Martin Cohos Commons

Boyce Crescent NW
Bus: 4/5, 10, 19
C-Train: SAIT Station
Historic Building, Rest Area, View

Heritage Hall at SAIT

Description:
This open green space is located in front of Heritage Hall on the grounds of SAIT. Martin Cohos is associated with the architectural firm of Cohos Evamy Partners. He has been very involved with SAIT both as an instructor and on the board of governors.

History:

Heritage Hall is one of Calgary's outstanding heritage buildings. The building was constructed in 1922 and used by both the Provincial Institute of Technology and Art and by Calgary Normal School. The Royal Canadian Air Force took over the building in World War II for training purposes. The campus was renamed SAIT or Southern Alberta Institute of Technology in 1963. There is a National Historic Site plaque near the front doors.

Nearby Parks and Green Spaces:

Riley Park and Burns Memorial Gardens are a short walk away from the front of Heritage Hall.

Tom Campbell's Hill Park

Centre Avenue and 13th Street NE
Bus: 17, 19
C-Train: Zoo Station
Interpretive Plaques, Views, Walking

Entrance to park

Description:

This open park area is located just north of the Calgary Zoo on the north side of Memorial Drive. The park area includes the escarpment slopes on three sides and a flat area at the top of the escarpment. Before the construction of Memorial Drive and the C-Train tracks the top of the escarpment extended further south to end at a steep escarpment slope overlooking the river.

History:

On top of this former escarpment there was a large billboard facing south which advertised Tom Campbell's Hats. There are interpretive plaques at the top edge of the present day escarpment. One plaque has information on the origin of the park's name. Several of the plaques have information about grassland natural areas and also about the shaping of the landscape.

Information plaques at south end of park

Nearby Parks and Green Spaces:

The Calgary Zoo and Nose Creek Pathway are both

located close to this park.

Tuxedo Community Park

29th Avenue and 1st Street NE
Bus: 3
Ball Diamond, Community Hall, Outdoor Rink, Playground

Tuxedo is one of Calgary's older community parks

Description:
This park is another of Calgary's older community parks. There are numerous large trees in the park. On the south side of the park is Tuxedo School, one of Calgary's older school buildings.

History:
This park was developed prior to World War I. One of the early features in the park was a bandstand. The bandstand had been removed by 1930 and the park was used for football and hockey. There was also a children's

127

playground. In the 1930s there was a wading pool in the park.

The name Tuxedo Park probably comes from a location of the same name near the city of New York. In 1911, developers described Calgary's Tuxedo Park as a community which would feature beautiful gardens, wide streets and attractive boulevards.

Ukrainian Pioneers Park
8th Avenue and 6th Street NE
Bus: 17
Playground, Rest Area

Assumption of the Blessed Virgin Mary Ukrainian Catholic Church

Description:
This park was dedicated in 1991 to the memory of the first Ukrainian pioneers to arrive in Alberta in 1891. Across the road from the southeast corner of the park is Assumption of the Blessed Virgin Mary Ukrainian

Catholic Church.

History:
Adjacent to the northeast corner of the park is Stanley Jones School, a large sandstone building constructed in 1913. For a short time the building was named Bridgeland School but was renamed to honour Stanley Jones, a prominent Calgary lawyer killed in action in World War I.

Stanley Jones School

Area Five

The boundaries of this area are Memorial Drive on the south, Deerfoot Trail on the west and the city limits on the north and east. The districts located in this area are Abbeydale, Belfast, Castleridge, Coral Springs, Falconridge, Marlborough, Marlborough Park, Martindale, Mayland Heights, Monterey Park, Pineridge, Rundle, Saddleridge, Taradale, Temple, Vista Heights and Whitehorn.

"It is very desirable that properly organized children's playgrounds be formed in each of our parks."
- William Reader, Calgary Parks Superintendent, 1913

Prairie Winds Park

130

Area Five Map

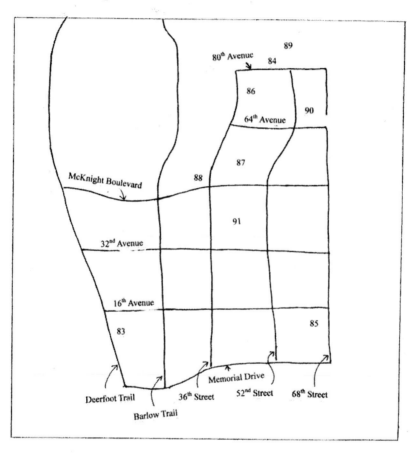

83. Deerfoot Athletic Park
84. Hugh Bennett Park
85. Marlborough Community
86. Martha's Haven Park
87. Prairie Winds Park

88. Rotary Challenger
89. Saddle Ridge Pond
90. Taradale Pond
91. Whitehorn Pathway

Deerfoot Athletic Park

16th Street and 14th Avenue NE
Bus: 19
Ball Diamonds, Picnic Tables, Playground, Soccer Field, Tennis Courts, Tobogganing

Description:
This park is sandwiched between Deerfoot Trail and the district of Mayland Heights. The north parking lot for the ball diamonds is accessed from 16th Street and 14th Avenue NE. The south parking lot is accessed from 8th Avenue NE. The south lot is closer to the tennis courts, playground, picnic tables and soccer field. Although the east side of the park has a slope, fences and trees at the bottom of the hill limit the area that can be used for tobogganing.

It can be very noisy in this park with the constant sound of traffic on Deerfoot Trail and at times the planes using the north-south runway.

Hugh Bennett Park

Saddlecreek Gate and Saddlecreek Way NE
Bus: 428
Bird Watching, Historic Plaque, Walking

Description:
This impressive wetlands is a great location for bird watchers to visit. One interesting feature of the wetlands is the narrow peninsulas of land that jut out into the pond area allowing for a potentially better view of the waterfowl. There is a paved path around the east side of the wetlands. The trail on the west side can be a bit muddy at times. In the north east corner of the pond, there is a constructed water feature with the water flowing over a series of small waterfalls into the pond. Along the edge of the water there are several interpretive plaques about either the district of Saddle Ridge or the

wetlands. Residences back onto almost the entire perimeter of the pond.

History:
At the south end of the wetlands is a small ornamental area dedicated to the memory of Hugh Bennett. He moved to this area with his family in 1929 at the age of 12. As a child Hugh attended Nose Creek School, a two room schoolhouse that was located near the present day intersection of McKnight Boulevard and Edmonton Trail. In 1968 Hugh became the first president of the Saddle Ridge Community Association.

In 1889 John Lewis became the first settler in this area. Later, his farm was successfully worked by his daughter Belle.

Waterfall at the north end of Hugh Bennett Park

Marlborough Community Park

Madigan Drive and 5th Avenue NE
Bus: 42
Ball Diamonds, Community Hall, Cycling, Picnic Tables, Playgrounds, Skating, Soccer Fields, Tennis, Tobogganing, Walking

Description:
This large community park shares green space with Roland Michener School, St. Martha's School and Dr. Gladys Egbert School. Most of the park is open area. Trees planted when the park was developed have grown substantially. The community hall is located on the east side of the park.

A large section of the park has been dug out to make a dry pond area. The slopes around the dry pond can be used as short toboggan slopes. In the winter a large skating area is located in the dry pond.

Looking west across the park

Martha's Haven Park
Martindale Boulevard and Martha's Haven Park
Bus: 428
Sculpture

Description:
   In this community park there is a sculpture entitled *"At Home in Martha's Haven"*. The sculpture depicts an adult pushing a child on a swing with a dog nearby. A sign indicates the sculpture was placed here in 1998 by Hopewell Residential Communities. There are no other facilities in this park.

Sculpture in park

Prairie Winds Park

223 Castleridge Boulevard NE
Bus: 21, 55
Ball Diamond, Changing Rooms, Playground, Skating, Soccer Field, Tennis Courts, Tobogganing, Wading Pool, Walking, Washrooms

Description:
This large regional park is on the west side of the Castleridge district. The official opening was in the fall of 1990. A plaque recognizes the community and volunteer efforts of area residents who played a huge part in the development of the park. Local school children participated in a contest to name the park. The winning name was selected by representatives from the city and community.

The large wading pool area of the park is very popular on hot summer days. This park is certainly a wonderful oasis in an area of Calgary that could use more green space.

Prairie Winds Park

As Westwinds Business Park has developed it has surrounded the park on three sides.

A paved path leads to small gazebo on top of a small hill at the west end of the park. Nearby is Grant MacEwan Grove, an area of ninety trees dedicated by the city on the occasion of J. W. Grant MacEwan's 90th birthday in 1992. He was an important author writing over thirty books about Western Canada. In civic life, he served as a Calgary alderman from 1953 to 1963. He was mayor of Calgary from 1963 to 1966. After serving as a Liberal MLA and provincial Liberal leader he was appointed Lieutenant Governor of the province. He held this position from 1966 to 1974.

Path leading to Prairie Winds Park wading pool

Rotary Challenger Park

East on 48th Avenue from Barlow Trail NE
Bus: No regular service
Ball Diamond, Playground, Sculpture, Tennis Courts, Washrooms

Description:
This park is the home of Special Olympics in Calgary. At the time of writing some of the park's facilities have not been completed. The facilities include two buildings that can be used by visitors.

Visitors to the park must make arrangements to use the facilities.

Saddle Ridge Pond

Saddlecrest Boulevard NE
Bus: 428
Basketball, Bird Watching, Playground, Walking

Looking west at Saddle Ridge Pond

Description:
At the time of writing there is a walking path that goes

partway around the edge of this L-shaped pond. The area to the west of the pond has not been developed and is still an open field.

A playground and one basketball hoop are located in the park. Time can also be spent sitting on a bench watching the waterfowl.

Taradale Pond
Taravista Drive
Bus: 436
Bird Watching, Walking

Taradale Pond and Gazebo

Description:
At the time of writing this district is still being developed. The pond is hidden away amongst the residences in the northwest corner of Taradale. This is a great location for anyone looking for a new spot for a short walk. There is a paved path which circles around the pond, past the houses that back onto the water.

139

At the west end of the pond there is a pleasant rest area with a gazebo-like structure and benches. On several visits to this pond, there have been numerous waterfowl making use of the site.

Whitehorn Pathway

Whitehorn Road NE
Bus: 72/73
Community Hall, Cycling, In-Line Skating, Playgrounds, Skating, Tennis Courts, Walking

Description:
A pathway leads through green space in this district. From the starting point by the community hall, you can walk east to 52nd Street. Please note that the Temple Pathway on the other side of 52nd Street is a bit difficult to follow. You can also walk west from the community hall to where the path splits. The path going south crosses 32nd Avenue into the Rundle district and passes through several school fields. The path going north extends to McKnight Boulevard. From here it is possible to follow a pathway through Westwinds Business Park to Prairie Winds Park.

It is possible to make a complete circuit on pathways through the four districts of the Properties. However it is suggested that pathway users carry a map as the route can be very confusing at times. In a couple of sections the route goes between houses and follows short sections of back alleys.

The outdoor rink beside the community hall has a paved surface, allowing for ball hockey games in the warmer weather.

Bibliography

Barraclough, Morris. *From Prairie to Park, Green Spaces in Calgary.* Calgary: Century Calgary Publications, 1975.

Bullick, Terry. *Calgary Parks and Pathways.* Calgary: Rocky Mountain Books, 1990.

Calgary Field Naturalists Society, Hallworth, Beryl, Editor. *Nose Hill A Popular Guide.* Calgary: Calgary Field Naturalists Society, 1988.

Humber, Donna Mae. *What's In A Name . . . Calgary?* Calgary: Detselig Enterprises Ltd., 1995.

Humber, Donna Mae. *What's In A Name . . . Calgary? Volume II.* Calgary: Detselig Enterprises Ltd., 1997.

Kwasny, Barbara., Peake, Elaine. *A Second Look at Calgary's Public Art.* Calgary: Detselig Enterprises Ltd., 1992.

Morgan, Brandt. *Enjoying Seattle's Parks.* Seattle: Greenwood Publications, 1979.

Sanders, Harry M. *Historic Walks of Calgary.* Calgary: Red Deer Press, 2005.

Tempelman-Kluit, Anne. *Green Spaces of Vancouver.* Vancouver: Brighouse Press, 1990.

Also by Peyto Lake Books

Walk Calgary's Escarpments and Bluffs by David Peyto.
Soft Cover, 6" by 9", 168 pages, 90 black and white photos, 55 black and white maps, 0-9731066-4-6, $16.95, 2005.

Banff Town Warden: The Journals of Walter H. Peyto, Rocky Mountains Park, Banff, 1914 to 1922, edited by David W. Peyto.
Soft Cover, 5.5" by 8.5", 242 pages, 35 black and white photos, 3 black and white maps, 0-9731066-0-3, $19.95, 2002

Banff Town Warden 2: The Journals of Walter H. Peyto, Rocky Mountains Park, Banff, 1923 to 1928, edited by David W. Peyto.
Soft Cover, 5.5" by 8.5", 260 pages, 29 black and white photos, 3 black and white maps, 0-9731066-3-8, $19.95, 2004.

Bill Peyto Guide to Canadian Rockies Trivia - Volume 1 by David W. Peyto.
Soft Cover, 6" by 9", 125 pages, 0-9731066-1-1, $10.00, 2003.

Bill Peyto Guide to Canadian Rockies Trivia - Volume 2 by David W. Peyto.
Soft Cover, 6" by 9", 121 pages, 0-9731066-2-X, $10.00, 2003.

Upcoming Publications

Banff Town Warden 3, 1929 to 1934

Discover Southwest Calgary's Parks and Green Spaces

Discover Southeast Calgary's Parks and Green Spaces

About the Author

David Peyto is a retired elementary school physical education teacher. His interests include walking and exploring the parks and green spaces of Calgary.